7 Si
Ste
Uncl
You

7 Simple Steps to Unclutter Your Life

Donna Smallin

STOREY
BOOKS

Schoolhouse Road
Pownal, Vermont 05261

The mission of Storey Communications is to serve our customers
by publishing practical information that encourages personal
independence in harmony with the environment.

Edited by Deborah Balmuth and Robin Catalano
Cover design by Meredith Maker
Cover and interior illustrations by Carleen Powell
Text design by Susan Bernier
Text production by Jennifer Jepson Smith
Indexed by Peggy Holloway, Holloway Indexing Services

The information in this book is true and complete to the best
of our knowledge. All recommendations are made without guar-
antee on the part of the author or Storey Books. The author and
publisher disclaim any liability in connection with the use of this
information. For additional information, please contact Storey
Books, Schoolhouse Road, Pownal, Vermont 05261.

Storey books are available for special premium and promotional
uses and for customized editions. For further information, please
call Storey's Custom Publishing Department at 1-800-793-9396.

Printed in the United States
ISBN 0-7394-0780-5

Contents

Dedication

For Mom and Dad,
who turned out all right after all.

Acknowledgments

Many thanks to my research assistant, Monica Schurr, who unearthed excellent reference materials, tracked down obscure details, and generously contributed her own ideas. I also want to thank my husband and family (especially you, Gramma), for inspiring and encouraging me to live a simpler life. Special thanks go to my publisher for giving me this opportunity to share what I have learned, and to Robin Catalano, my editor, for pulling it together so beautifully.